Books by M. Blaine Smith

REACH BEYOND YOUR GRASP: Embracing Dreams That Reflect God's Best for You—And Achieving Them

MARRY A FRIEND: Finding Someone to Marry Who Is Truly Right for You

EMOTIONAL INTELLIGENCE FOR THE CHRISTIAN

THE YES ANXIETY: Taming the Fear of Commitment

OVERCOMING SHYNESS: Conquering Your Social Fears

ONE OF A KIND: A Biblical View of Self-Acceptance

FAITH AND OPTIMISM: Positive Expectation in the Christian Life

KNOWING GOD'S WILL: Finding Guidance for Personal Decisions

SHOULD I GET MARRIED?

Goal Setting

for the

Christian

Harnessing
the Stunning Benefits
of Focus and Persistence
to Realize Your Potential
for Christ—and Your
God-Given Dreams

M. Blaine Smith

SilverCrest
B•O•O•K•S

Library of Congress Control Number: 2001012345

ISBN: 978-0-9840322-7-3

Contents

Author's Note

Chapter one of this book ("Ten Steps to a Life-Changing Goal") is excerpted from my *Reach Beyond Your Grasp: Embracing Dreams That Reflect God's Best for You—And Achieving Them*. I consider it the most important chapter of that book, and following the strategy it outlines for setting an effective goal will hugely increase your potential for achieving a goal or dream that God has inspired within you.

Chapters two and three focus on the remarkable value of persevering toward a goal or dream till you achieve it. Chapter two ("The Triumph of Simple Persistence") looks at the extreme and often surprising benefits of persistence, and how with sufficient time—and relaxed effort—"impossible" goals can be achieved.

Chapter three ("Not So Fast with 'Closed Doors'"!) considers the question of God's will in relation to this persisting: Do we reach a point when certain failures or setbacks indicate God is telling us to abandon a dream? Here, again, the answer is often surprising and reassuring. The setback may simply "go with the territory" in pursuing the goal, and with further effort, we'll succeed. Or God may be nudging us to a mid-course correction—which, with further persistence will make all the difference in our success.*

This is purposely a short book, to get you up-and-running with the goal setting process. If you want a broader

*Part of chapter three is adapted from my *Faith and Optimism* (formerly *The Optimism Factor*).

discussion of realizing personal goals and dreams, please see my *Reach Beyond your Grasp*.

The Proverbs give us a time-honored and indisputable promise: "The plans of the diligent lead to profit as surely as haste leads to poverty" (Prov 21:5). We can certainly substitute "goals" for "plans" in this statement. We're told that in God's design of human life, we have the potential for significant accomplishment—far greater than we probably realize. Yet it requires careful planning, and firm commitment to the plans we make. That gets to the heart of this book.

Whoever you are, God has given you gifts that are an incomparable treasure and the potential to make a substantial difference. The secret lies in setting effective goals, then maintaining a reasonable pace toward them. My strong hope is that this book will give you the perspective to get your goals and dreams in motion, and the heart to stay on course till you achieve them!

1

Ten Steps to
a Life-Changing Goal

In MAY 1999 MY MOM CAME DOWN with rheumatoid arthritis almost overnight, then was diagnosed with chronic leukemia. By July this happily independent, gregarious 86-year-old required round-the-clock nursing, and seldom ventured from her second-story bedroom.

The cost of full-time nursing was devastating. Mom also longed for more activity and contact with people, but her body would no longer cooperate.

Assisted living was the obvious answer. For months Evie and I dragged our feet, though, certain that Mom wouldn't want to leave her beloved home of 44 years.

By January we had reached at least one conclusion: an assisted living facility near our home was far and away the best option for her. We met with a director there. They could take Mom eventually, she explained, but had a six-month waiting list, and then no guarantee of space.

Then something snapped inside us. Six months was too long to wait, given Mom's personal and financial needs. We set a goal—to have her happily moved out of her home and into a better arrangement by the end of February. I stress *happily,* for we weren't going to force her, but would do whatever we could to encourage a welcome transition.

Almost immediately we recognized a solution we'd missed before. To this point we'd assumed we had no space to host her in our home, even for a short time. Now it occurred to us that we could convert our upstairs family room into a temporary guest room, until her apartment was ready.

Option one.

Then dawned option two. It was far more preferable, but seemed highly improbable. *What if?* I wondered. *What if the door that seems presently closed at the assisted living home has a crack?*

In that nothing-ventured, nothing-gained spirit that only a goal can inspire, I phoned the director, and explained to her that we really needed to move my mom out of her home soon. Did they possibly have a way to accommodate her temporarily, until her own unit comes available? I was stunned when she replied that she'd look into it.

Several days later she phoned back to say they had a guest suite available that Mom could rent for as long as necessary. And the charge for it was less than for permanent residency.

Now the job of convincing Mom. We were equally stunned to find that she needed no persuading. She was ready to move and eager for a new adventure.

On February 25, 2000, we moved her in to this haven, where she lived very happily—soon in her own apartment—until her death in July 2003. The improvements to her social life, health and finances were remarkable.

What a Difference a Goal Makes

This surely isn't the most dramatic story you've heard about goal setting. Our situation wasn't desperate. It wouldn't have been a calamity if we'd had to wait six months or longer to move Mom into assisted living. Still, we were faced with a situation that was far from desirable, and wanted a way to improve it. Once we set a goal, things changed quickly.

The goal substantially influenced how Evie and I thought about our predicament. Our minds started working. We saw possibilities we hadn't recognized before. It also gave me the resolve to broach an option with the director of the home that I wouldn't have considered raising otherwise. After all, if they had temporary housing, she surely would have said so during our long interview. Yet simply asking the question made all the difference.

I'm certain, too, that the sense of urgency I conveyed when I phoned her affected her response, and her decision to explore an option at her mammoth facility that she normally wouldn't have mentioned. Our goal influenced the outcome.

There's no question, either, that the excitement Evie and I felt about this sudden open door was contagious to Mom. Had we been less focused, and less convinced, she would have been less certain about wanting to move.

This story demonstrates how goal setting can help us resolve moderately challenging problems—the type we often try to tackle head-first without first establishing a clear goal. The same dynamics that worked for Evie and me in this case will work for any of us in setting more far-reaching goals to achieve our major life dreams. Nothing helps us more to accomplish a dream than having well-conceived goals. A major dream may require us to set a variety of goals of different dimensions en route to reaching it. The good news is that any of us can greatly improve our ability to set goals effectively, and, with them in place, can radically increase our potential for reaching our dream.

The Power of Focused Intentions

Pick up any book on human potential, positive thinking or the secrets of success, and you'll likely find the author extolling the benefits of goal setting. You may well find the writer declaring that an effectively-set goal *guarantees* your success.

I'd caution that life offers no guarantees. Even our best-laid plans never assure any outcome beyond question. If you set out tomorrow at 11:00 a.m. to drive from Baltimore, Maryland to Columbus, Ohio, determined to meet a friend for dinner at 6:00 p.m., there's no promise you'll make it. Your car may break down. You may have an accident. You may encounter weather problems or traffic delays. You may suffer a heart attack, and make it neither to Columbus nor back home.

Life offers no guarantees.

Still, it's likely you will make your goal. If your car is in good running order, you know the route and exercise reasonable prudence, the odds are overwhelming you'll reach Columbus by 6:00 p.m. You can tell your friend you'll meet her, and proceed with confidence that you'll keep your commitment.

A properly-set goal in any area assures your success with similar probability. Probability so high that you can go forward with the conviction that, Lord willing, you'll accomplish your objective. Such confidence isn't audacious or brazen, but simply respects how God has designed human life to function.

With a major, long-term goal, you'll probably make some adjustments in the deadline as you move along, to be sure. You'll modify some aspects of your goal as well. Still, the likelihood you'll achieve your *primary* objective is very high, providing you've carefully set your goal to begin with, and your passion for reaching it remains strong.

The parallel to a road trip is helpful from another angle. If you're like me, you enjoy driving. Sure, it takes effort and focused attention. Yet it's much less arduous, say, than laying cinder block or studying for a physics final. You may grow tired while driving, need to rest and regain your energy. Yet most of the time it's fun, and seems natural and effortless.

When you're living out a goal that's well conceived, and truly right for you, you feel much the same way. Far from requiring heroic self-discipline, the goal taps your natural motivation, and moves you forward at a pace that works for you. You may get tired or encounter obstacles, just as you would on a road trip. Yet, overall, the process is enjoyable— in part because you're fueled by natural energy, in part because you're excited about your destination.

How Goals Help Us
Let's look more specifically at the benefits goals bring us.

There are at least eight ways in which they help us achieve our objectives and dreams.

1. Goals break the inertia. Inertia is the single greatest barrier to our achieving a dream. A body at rest stays at rest. Yet a body in motion stays in motion—and so anything we can do to get our life moving toward a desired outcome is beneficial. Monumental challenges, which seem beyond our capacity and strength, suddenly feel surprisingly manageable once we begin to tackle them. Goals break the inertia, by giving us the incentive to take that first step.

2. Goals give us occasions to rise to. Dale Carnegie observed that our most deep-seated human need is to be important. We each long to be doing notable things with our life, and we instinctively give the best of our time and attention to those tasks we consider most important. A goal lets us draw on this natural energy, by allowing us to determine in advance that a particular objective truly is worth our most earnest effort. Once we've established that fact, the goal gives us an occasion to aspire to, providing the most effective possible motivation to keep us in motion.

3. Goals focus our thinking and energy. Nature abounds with energy sources of unspeakable potential that vastly increase their benefit when harnessed and focused in strategic ways. A gently flowing river, dammed and forced to flow through a small channel, produces a ferocious output, capable of turning the wheels of a power plant providing electricity to an entire city.

Goals have a similar effect on our mental energy, enabling us to accomplish exceedingly more than is possible without them. Most important, goals harness our subconscious energy. They serve our subconscious notice that specific problems need to be solved, and enlist the most creative partner in our mental process as an ally. Before we know it, insightful answers begin to emerge that we've never considered.

We see an enlightening example of how a goal can ignite creativity in a familiar Gospel incident. Four men have a goal—to bring a paralyzed friend to Jesus for healing (Mk 2:1-12). They carry him on a pallet to a house where he's teaching, only to find that they cannot move him through the huge, dense crowd overflowing the home. Rather than accept defeat, they look for a solution, finding an unlikely one. Instead of going through the crowd, they'll go above it! They climb to the roof, remove tiles over the section of the home where Jesus is speaking, then lower the pallet carrying their friend through that opening—compelling Jesus' attention.

Far from being offended by their aggressiveness, Jesus is impressed with their faith (v. 5). He forgives the man's sins, then heals his paralysis.

What's fascinating about this incident is that these men, in their mutual determination, conceived a solution to a problem that most would have considered unsolvable. Had they been less determined and focused, I doubt that their minds would have worked as well. Inertia would have prevailed. They would have settled for sitting placidly in the back of the crowd as spectators, failing to seize the golden opportunity before them. The fact that they had a clear agenda sparked their creativity, and inspired an ingenious solution to a difficult predicament.

Goals stimulate our own problem-solving skills in a similar fashion. They also heighten our alertness to opportunities we'd otherwise miss.

4. Goals inspire others to help us. We each have a natural instinct to be generous and helpful to others. A goal that we set for ourselves best allows us to appeal to this instinct in others, for it provides evidence to them that their effort to help us will be worthwhile. It also signals to them what sort of assistance we may need, and helps them recognize more readily how they can support us. Goals enable us to appeal to another instinct in others as well—the desire to root for someone who is making an honest effort to improve their life.

Setting a goal also helps us clarify in our own mind what sort of help we need to seek from others, and strengthens our courage to ask for it.

5. Goals open us more fully to God's help and provision. Well-set goals are an exercise in stewardship—stewardship of the life God has called us to live. It only makes sense that God will more likely extend his help to us when we're treating the life he has entrusted to us responsibly. The help God provides to those who set responsible goals seems to be part of his common grace; human potential writers, for instance, often speak of "synchronicity" or "serendipities" that occur when a goal has been set—fortuitous coincidences that help you realize your objective.

How much more should we expect special help from God when, as a follower of Christ, we have set a goal prayerfully, seeking his direction and provision. The goal also increases our alertness to windows of opportunity God may be opening.

6. Goals increase both our confidence and motivation to carry out all of the details necessary to achieve them.

The best-set goal includes a clear plan of action, describing what work will be done when. Because we have such a blueprint in place, we're able to give our full attention to any of its details, knowing that the time and space is there to accomplish the other steps when necessary. We work more confidently on any segment of our plan, for we're not worrying that we're robbing time from more important tasks. We're also more likely to enjoy the less-scintillating steps necessary to achieve a dream, for we recognize how they are moving us toward an objective we dearly want to accomplish.

7. Goals give us a basis for measurable results. Our plan of action also enables us to better judge whether specific work we're doing is actually helping us accomplish our objective. We're better able to work smarter, and to take corrective action when needed.

8. Goals give us something to celebrate. Because a goal gives us a clearly defined target, we know when we've hit it. We now have something specific and meaningful to celebrate. This jubilant occasion is not only a tonic to us when it occurs, but another carrot-on-a-stick aspect of a goal, beckoning us to see it through to the finish.

Setting Goals Successfully

Appreciating the benefits goals provide helps us greatly to find the incentive to set them. How, then, do we do this effectively? Goal setting is more of an art than a science, to be sure. The process that most helps you may differ from what works for me. Each of us needs to experiment to find what steps benefit us most personally. Still, there are certain approaches to goal setting that universally help people turn dreams into reality. Here are ten of the most important principles to keep in mind.

1. Goals should be based on strong desire. The most common reason goals fail is because we don't desire their results strongly enough.

Let's say I set a goal to become an accomplished pianist in five years. I may establish it for a variety of reasons. At one extreme, I may be motivated by intense desire: I passionately wish to be musical, crave the thrill of performing, or long for certain social benefits this skill may open.

At the other extreme, I may take on this goal more out of obligation. Perhaps I've long felt I have some potential to play piano, and that I owe it to myself to develop it. Or I may have some legitimate desire to be a pianist, yet underneath have a much greater yearning to become an actor. We set many goals primarily for the momentary relief of guilt that establishing them brings, but not because we earnestly long for their results.

We need to be thoroughly honest about our level of passion in considering a goal of this magnitude. If I strongly desire to become a competent pianist, chances are good I'll succeed. If I'm setting this goal mainly out of obligation, or as a substitute for a more burning creative desire, it's unlikely I'll stick with it past the fifth piano lesson.

Goals should spring as fully as possible from deep-seated natural motivation. Basing them on such desire isn't taking the course of least resistance, but is a matter of stewardship, for even the most intense motivation remains unproductive unless focused through a goal. If I need to set a goal for an outcome I'm less than exuberant about, I should first do what I can to boost my desire for that result. Apart from keen motivation, I shouldn't waste my time pursuing a goal. If the goal is required for reaching a major dream, then I should constantly bring to mind my exhilaration for the dream and remind myself how this goal fits into the bigger picture of my life.

2. *Goals should be achievable.* Goals should also fall clearly within our range of potential. Again, this isn't taking the course of least resistance, for goals stretch us to grow in ways that would never happen otherwise. Consider, too, that we each have vast possibilities for accomplishment within our areas of potential that will never be realized apart from concentrated effort. It only makes sense to choose our goals from this huge pool of options rather than from outside of it.

We should be confident also that we can relate temperamentally to the process necessary for achieving a goal. Not that we have to find all aspects of it scintillating. But if, for instance, I know that I'd find the regimen of practice necessary to become a competent pianist repugnant, I shouldn't lock in to this goal. *Some* enjoyment of the process in this case is important.

3. *Goals should be specific.* Goals should be clearly stated, both in terms of what we choose to accomplish, and the date when we plan to reach our target. Staying open-ended at either of these points greatly reduces the possibility that we'll achieve our objective.

4. *Goals should involve a clearly-defined plan of action.* One of the greatest benefits of goal setting is that it allows us to take charge of our life. We're able to peer into the future and lay claim to the time and process that will ensure our success. Even goals that seem impossible for us often can be achieved, if we allow enough time to reach them and plan our steps wisely.

It's unlikely we'll be able to predict every step required to accomplish a major goal in advance. Some of the details will only emerge as we move forward. Still, we should do our best to predict the most important steps, and then determine how and when we'll take them. The more fully we can develop a map for the journey ahead, the more likely we are to reach our destination.

The single most important part of this planning is to decide specifically when we'll invest the time needed for taking the different steps required for reaching our goal, so we can protect it as fully as possible. Start by determining, as best as you can, how much total time you'll need. Then consider when, in light of your energy and creative flow, are your *best* times for pursuing your objective—daily, weekly, monthly, yearly. Look also at what other commitments you'll need to rearrange or cancel to make way for this time. Design a schedule, even if it covers many years, which allows sufficient quality time for accomplishing your dream. Carving out this time, and guarding it as sacred, will make all the difference in hitting your target.

5. Goals should be established in prayer. While anyone can profit from goal setting, regardless of their spiritual orientation, we who understand the power of prayer have an unparalleled advantage in planning our future. Through it we're able to connect directly with the heart of God, and enjoy the supreme benefits that result.

When setting a major goal, we do best to give some generous time to prayer. We should ask God to direct our thinking, to help us understand the desires and gifts he has given us that most deserve our attention, and to make the wisest choice of a goal among the many options before us. Just as important, we should ask him to give us courage to move forward with what he is prompting us to do. We should also ask him to help us determine a clear strategy for carrying out our goal.

Once our goal is established, we should commit it to Christ, in the spirit of Proverbs 16:3. Prayer, of course, should not end at this point. We should continue to seek God's direction and strength as we move ahead, asking him daily to show us any changes or mid-course corrections we need to make. It's here that goal setting can have the auxiliary benefit of deepening our relationship with Christ, by allowing us to experience his companionship in the great adventures of our life.

6. Goals should be flexible. Once we've established the process and deadline for achieving a goal, we should assume these details are realistic and follow them earnestly and confidently. Yet we should also recognize in humility that we don't know the future—how circumstances will unfold, or what doors God may open for us. Our understanding of our own potential is always evolving as well. There's no shame, as we move ahead, in changing the deadline for a goal, rethinking some of its specifics, or even dropping the goal itself if we find it no longer fits our life as we now understand it. Such revising goes with the territory, even in the most competent goal setting.

In 1997, my Christian band Sons of Thunder set a goal to produce a new album—our first in 25 years. Our plan was to accomplish this task with a $10,000 budget, three days of recording and three days of mixing, and to have a CD available by June 1998. The first shipment of CDs finally arrived on Christmas Eve of that year. By then, we had spent nearly $40,000, and made nearly 20 additional visits to the studio beyond what we'd planned. Still, there's not the slightest question that the album would still be a wish dream apart from our having had a firm goal, which galvanized these widely dispersed musicians and singers—spread out in eight cities around the United States—to accomplish a task we at first thought inconceivable.

The adjustments you have to make in pursuing a major goal may not be nearly as extreme as this. Still, you'll probably find it necessary, even with the best-laid plan, to make some revision in the timing and process as you move along. Yet you will hit your primary target, if you don't lose heart—and that's the important thing. And the fact that you have a goal will make all the difference in what you're able to accomplish.

7. Goals should be written down. Take time to record your goal and plan of action in writing. Articulate the details as precisely as you can. The process of writing helps greatly to clarify your thinking, and provides a reliable record when your memory lags. Apart from putting the specifics in writing, we limit the effectiveness of a goal—far more than we usually realize.

8. Goals should be rehearsed. We possess no ability—natural or learned—that doesn't atrophy when unused. Our ability to walk diminishes if we're bedridden only a short time. We should treat goals as we do our most cherished skills. We should "practice" them—that is, rehearse and reclaim them often. Most important, we need to rekindle our motivation for them frequently.

We should do this daily with a major goal. Take time to

pray over such a goal each day. You may find it helpful to read over your written resolution, or recite it aloud. Visualize yourself succeeding. Imagine it's the day that you've finally achieved your goal; you're thinking back over all the time and effort you've invested to reach this point, immensely glad you never gave up. You're looking forward to a big celebration. Enjoy the exhilaration of this image for a moment. Then pray, asking God to help you make it a reality.

9. Goals should involve accountability and enlist cheerleaders. Most of us take great encouragement from knowing others are rooting for us to reach a goal. We benefit considerably from being accountable to others as well. Enlist your cheering squad—even if it's just one individual. Ask this person, or these people, to pray for you and encourage you as you work toward your goal, and make a pledge to them that you'll stay faithful to your intentions. Draw on their support as you move forward. And, of course, celebrate your victory with them when your mission is accomplished!

10. Goals should be celebrated! There's nothing unprofound in saying that we should celebrate a goal once we've reached it. In our driven nature, we can easily bypass time devoted purely to enjoying our achievement, out of zeal to move on to new projects. In devising a plan of action for a goal, we ought to plan in time for celebrating—not only our final victory, but also intermediate triumphs along the way. Knowing these occasions for rejoicing are in place will increase our incentive to move toward our goal. They will also give us special opportunity to thank God for what he has enabled us to accomplish—and, most important, to *feel* thankful to him, and to grasp in our heart as fully as possible all that he has done for us.

Goal setting should add a substantial element of joy to our life, for we're taking action to improve our life, and to harness our creative potential much more constructively. The hope for this joy is an important incentive to move forward.

Experiencing this joy is also critical, for it deepens our gratitude to God, enhances our health, and boosts our productivity and the benefit of our life to others. Planning times simply to experience such elation isn't frivolous, but part of the process that will best enable our life to be a channel of God's grace to the world.

Reaping the Benefits

Goal setting, more than any other factor, holds the key to achieving our important dreams. Appreciating this point is extraordinarily encouraging, for it means recognizing that God has given us much greater control over our destiny than we normally suppose.

If you have a dream that isn't moving forward well, let me encourage you to break it down into manageable goals. Give *serious* time to doing this, even if it takes many hours or days. Make it your initial goal to come up with a set of achievable goals that will move you successfully to your dream. Devote yourself earnestly to the process of setting them, and stay with that process until these goals are firmly established.

Then set out on the journey of accomplishing them one by one, keeping your eventual goal of reaching your dream firmly in mind. You'll likely revise your goals and their deadlines at many points as you move ahead. But the important thing is that your life is now in motion. You're giving God much greater freedom to direct and redirect you as well. With this map in place, you're far more likely to reach your destination.

Persistence

I want now to give some close attention to one more matter that can make or defeat us once we've carefully established a goal. And that's our need for staying optimistic and persistent for as long as necessary to achieve our objective. Even when we've set a goal for all the right reasons—it fits us well, and we deeply desire the results—we can lose heart too quickly over certain setbacks, or even conclude incorrectly that they signify God is nixing our plans. It helps us tremendously to understand that, in how God has designed human life, persisting through some difficult challenges is usually necessary to achieve our most important aspirations. To say it more positively—what we can accomplish through such perseverance greatly exceeds what we can achieve without it. And this higher potential for achievement-through-persistence should be appreciated as a special gift of God in itself, for it opens a whole new world of possibilities for us. This will be our focus of interest in the final two chapters.

2

The Triumph
of Simple Persistence

DURING THE CALIFORNIA GOLD RUSH a prospector named R. U. Darby helped his uncle mine a vein of gold that the latter had discovered. It appeared at first that they had a prosperous find. Yet the vein soon disappeared, and Darby and his uncle searched frantically for the spot where it continued. Finally, they concluded their prospects were hopeless and sold their equipment to a junk dealer.

The junk dealer consulted an engineer, then began mining the shaft again. He quickly discovered the elusive vein and a supply of gold worth millions of dollars—just three feet from where Darby and his uncle had stopped digging.[1]

The story brings to mind how our important battles in life are often won by simple persistence. It reminds us equally that we can give up on a goal too easily and are sometimes much closer to hitting our mark than we realize.

When we look at what made the accomplishments of notable individuals possible, we usually find persistence that went beyond the ordinary. Thomas Edison invented the incandescent light bulb only after thousands of failed attempts. He remarked, "The trouble with other inventors is that they try a few things and quit. I never quit until I get what I want."[2]

Ernest Hemingway's writing communicates so naturally that we might assume the Nobel laureate always got it right the first time. In truth, Hemingway reworked his material extensively, revising most novels five times, and *The Old Man and the Sea* more than two hundred times.

Soichiro Honda was also a master of persistence. The founder of Honda Motors and perfecter of the catalytic engine explained to a Michigan graduating class: "To me success can be achieved only through repeated failure and introspection. In fact, my success represents the one percent of the work that resulted from the ninety-nine percent that was called failure."[3]

We might imagine that underlying important accomplishment is usually dogged, backbreaking effort. More typically, the secret lies in *consistent* effort. Victory comes to those who stay with a dream long enough to reach it. End of story. In so many cases this patient plodding overrides serious limitations in ability, education or resources. Honda developed his automotive company and pioneered major engineering innovations with only eight years of formal education and meager financial backing.

Persistence plays such a compensating role in endless areas of human achievement. Research shows, for instance, that drilling companies which discover the most oil are not the ones with the best equipment or the most talented personnel—but those that dig the most wells.

In real life as most of us lead it, we often find we're unable to accomplish a goal within the time period we've envisioned. Yet when we're willing to revise our assumptions about time and deadlines, we succeed. I'm often moved by the examples of people who find a good opportunity for marriage well into their adult years. In every case they are those who, in spite of many disappointments, have stayed hopeful and open to new opportunities well beyond a point that many would consider reasonable. Often they continued doing the same things they had been doing for years to meet people—attending singles meetings and accepting blind dates—until they finally found a relationship that worked. Most will admit the temptation to give up had been strong. They are now exceedingly glad they persisted and never fully lost heart.

Healthy and Unhealthy Persistence

This isn't to say there is magic in persistence per se. We've got to persist at doing the right things. If our goal or our approach isn't sound to begin with, persistence will work against us. Saul of Tarsus persecuted Christians with merciless persistence; only in time did he discover that he was kicking "against the goads" (Acts 26:14). Yet Paul's tenacious personality remained strongly intact as a Christian and contributed immensely to the spread of the gospel. Paul opened more new regions for the gospel than anyone else— far and away—simply because he tried and never gave up. If one group or city wouldn't receive his message, he moved on to the next, and kept knocking on doors till one opened.

While Paul's success in evangelizing demonstrates the value of persistence, his persecution of Christians before his conversion shows its negative side and offers us a caution. If we've made an earnest effort to accomplish a goal yet are failing at every turn, we ought to look carefully at whether the goal isn't right for us or if there is a fatal flaw in our approach. Occasionally we'll find that, like Paul, we need to make a radical change in direction. At other times we'll find that an incremental change in approach makes all the difference.

In other cases—a surprising number for some of us—we'll discover that we're wisest to stay the course. The most important step we can take in resolving this question is to get the best counsel available to us. Had R. U. Darby merely sought expert opinion, as the junk dealer did, he would have found that he didn't understand the fault lines in the mine shaft, which indicated that gold was present just a short distance away. Through the help of others' counsel, we often make this same gratifying discovery: The problem is neither with our goal nor our approach, but we're misreading life's "fault lines." If we'll keep doing exactly what we're doing, we'll succeed; we only need to revise our expectations about time.

Persistence is often preached as a virtue—an obligation of maturity: "Stick with your studies, son, and you'll earn that degree and make something of your life." Yet, much more important, we ought to understand persistence as a *benefit* to our life as God has designed it. It is often the key to reaching cherished goals and to solving "impossible" problems. While it may seem undramatic to say that slow and steady wins the race, the truth is that many more battles in life are won by patient plodding than through ingenious solutions or miraculous breakthroughs.

Vertical and Horizontal Time

The point is encouraging to keep in mind not only when we face obstacles in reaching goals but when we're establishing them in the first place. We often write dreams off as infeasible for us that we actually could accomplish with enough time.

In *The Magic Lamp: Goal Setting for People Who Hate Setting Goals,* an outstanding book on setting personal goals, Keith Ellis makes a distinction between "vertical time" and "horizontal time."[4] Vertical time is that period just ahead of us—the day we are in and our immediate future. Horizontal time is the period that extends indefinitely into the future. We can accomplish certain goals in vertical time; with heroic effort of will, we may occasionally do impressive things—run a marathon in an afternoon, write a major term paper in one day, respond to a crisis that requires sacrificing sleep for a night or two. Yet we're unable to run at such high velocity indefinitely; we carry out most of our important accomplishments in horizontal time, and not through spectacular effort but one half-step at a time.

The distinction on the one hand is maddeningly simple. Of course we all realize we can accomplish more through patient long-term perseverance than through manic effort in the present; we've known that ever since reading *The Tortoise and the Hare* in kindergarten. Yet having this fresh vocabulary for speaking of the time available to us is helpful, for it aids both our self-talk and our visualization. It inspires us to think more creatively about what our possibilities might be if we allowed ourselves the luxury of all the time necessary—even with very small steps—to accomplish a goal. We need all the incentive we can get for such long-range dreaming, for the emphasis on instant gratification in our culture inclines us to do the opposite—to focus on what we can accomplish quickly, then to grow discouraged over how limited our options seem to be.

It is often stunning to realize what we can accomplish with the benefit of horizontal time, by breaking a goal down to manageable steps. Need to write a book of two hundred pages? Sound impossible? One paragraph a day for a year will do it—or several sentences a day for two years. Need to take a graduate program with twenty courses? Two courses a year for ten years will get you through—or four courses for five.

Ellis is a prophet for horizontal time, enamored with what we can achieve in life without grueling effort, by merely moving along at our own pace. The concept is a redemptive one, for it helps us to appreciate the time available to us in one lifetime as an unspeakable gift of God and to see practical possibilities for our life we would otherwise miss.

In Ellis's own words: "Given enough horizontal time, you can learn to play a musical instrument, master a foreign language, read the collected works of William Shakespeare, dig yourself a swimming pool, earn a college degree, build an addition on your house, learn a trade, write a book, land a new job, start a company, or all of the above. It might take you a year, or it might take you twenty years—so what?"[5]

Going the Distance—At Your Pace
Appreciating our potential in horizontal time gives us the

courage to set goals, even very long-term ones. By setting a carefully conceived goal and embracing it wholeheartedly, we vastly increase our potential for success.

Paul succeeded in his mission and found the heart to persevere through shipwrecks and stonings, because his intention to be a groundbreaker for the gospel was so clearly focused. "[I have made] it my ambition to preach the gospel, not where Christ has already been named," he explained (Rom 15:20 RSV). Paul wasn't implying that every Christian must have his specific ambition of bringing the gospel to unevangelized people; his was an intensely personal one, springing from an understanding of his gifts and God's unique plan for him. When Paul taught on individual mission, he stressed that Christians should look to the gifts, desires and opportunities that God has given them personally (Rom 12: 3-8, 1 Cor 12, Eph 4:4-16). Yet he demonstrated by his example the extreme benefit that comes from having clear goals based on these distinctives.

It helps us too, in finding the heart to set these goals, to remember assurances Jesus gave about our potential for being productive as his followers. He taught emphatically that he intends us to be productive, and that he gives us special help when we seek to invest our life productively. He went as far as to assure us that we will do "greater works" than he did (Jn 14:12). We seldom think about this astounding promise Jesus made, nor experience the motivation he intended it to inspire, for it is puzzling. How could any of us come close to matching the quality of his accomplishments?

Keith Ellis's distinction between the two types of time available to us helps in explaining what Jesus must have meant. Jesus certainly didn't mean that any of us could surpass the works he performed in vertical time. Even the most gifted healer among us could not match his degree of miraculous healing—which included raising the dead—nor could the most gifted evangelist impart salvation. Yet most of us have far more horizontal time available to us than Jesus allowed himself during his earthly mission. It's within this context that we have the possibility of a more substantial quantity of accomplishments—plus the potential for achievements that require considerable time and focus to carry out.

It's this thought—that God intends our life to be uniquely productive in horizontal time—that, more than anything else, can give us the courage to dream big and set challenging goals.

Our Critical Need to Think Big

In short, there can be no question that God wants us to think big about our future, and about the life he has entrusted to us. He wants us to treasure the time we have at our disposal, and to appreciate it as his greatest gift to us in earthly life—vertical time, to be sure, but especially horizontal time, with its amazing possibilities. And he wants us to manage this extended time in the wisest ways possible. This means seeing it as a matter of obedience to set certain well-conceived goals that allow us to harness our potential most effectively for Christ. But we should also realize that our greatest joy lies in pursuing these goals, for they trigger our hope, kindle our energy, give us focus—and through it all improve our health, vitality and mental health—and that's just through the process of carrying them out, not to mention the huge benefits they bring us by allowing us to achieve certain cherished objectives.

We even discover that the challenges and setbacks we experience in persisting toward these goals bring a welcome sense of adventure to our life, a sense of purpose as we tackle them, and unparalleled joy when we handle them successfully. And we discover that living at this level is far better than just sitting and whittling the time away.

And so the triumph of simple persistence comes not only in the results we achieve, but in the process of pursuing them as well!

Still, with all of this said, we can be dogged by questions of how much persistence is really honoring to Christ. Do we reach a point after a certain time, even with a goal that's carefully thought through and fits us well, when persistence indicates bullheadedness and not faith? Here we come to another reassuring distinction, which clarifies this question, and will be our focus in the next chapter.

3

Not So Fast
with "Closed Doors"!

I'll NEVER FORGET A STORY that made the national news some years ago. CNN announced as a headline item that a man had passed his bar exam. While passing the bar is a notable achievement, it doesn't normally attract the attention of the national media. Yet his case was unique, for this tenacious soul had failed the test forty-seven previous times. Now, at age sixty, he finally passed on his forty-eighth try.

That's not all. The man noted in an interview that he hoped to embark on a twenty-year career as an attorney. As proof of his earnestness, he had purchased a briefcase!

I must confess I have a soft spot in my heart for this gentleman, as eccentric as his case may be. I always find examples like his inspiring, for they bring to mind how some of us by nature are late bloomers—and that it's okay to be so. We run on different clocks. God has different timetables for each of us. While one person realizes a significant accomplishment early in life, another does so much later.

His example is extreme, unquestionably. We might conclude that he demonstrates stubbornness more than healthy determination and could have spent his energy in better ways. Still, it's hard not to admire his perseverance, which continued way beyond the point when most of us would have quit. Our human tendency is to go to the opposite extreme—to give up after a setback or two, even when a reasonable possibility of success still exists.

Faith generates optimism, and the person who walks in faith stays hopeful about reaching a goal as long as this expectation is justified. Resilience, too, is involved in genuine faith: we're able to rebound from loss and disappointment and regain our confidence about succeeding.

Yet for thoughtful Christians this raises a nagging question. Just when should you assume that a door is truly closed? At what point must you conclude that God wants you to let go of a longstanding desire and simply accept things as they are?

Easily Discouraged
To be honest, it takes little disappointment in any area for us to conclude that God is against our succeeding. I recall talking to a woman who deeply wanted to be married yet feared the opportunity had passed her by. Many of her friends had already married, and the one relationship that held the prospect of marriage for her had ended. She wondered if God was indicating through it all that she should abandon her

hope of marrying and set her heart on staying single. She was twenty-two.

Christians who move into their later twenties, thirties or beyond, wanting to be married but finding no suitable opportunity, are especially inclined to draw the conclusion that this young woman reached. They're even more likely to do so if they've experienced a number of broken relationships or rejections along the way. If you're in this position, it may seem in all sincerity that the most Christ-honoring, reverent assumption you can make is that God is telling you to forsake your hope for marriage. Surely obedience to him must require that you put this desire on the altar and learn to joyfully accept your singleness.

But then you witness an example that defies the norm. A friend, well into her adult years and survivor of many disappointments, suddenly and surprisingly finds an excellent opportunity for marriage. Once she is married and the dust clears, she declares that she is glad she never let go of her hope. She even claims that she sees value now in those past relationships that didn't work out, for through them she grew and developed the qualities that have allowed her finally to be happily married. God does indeed have different clocks for us, she insists; she's grateful for that and thankful that she waited.

And so you're thrown back to square one. Just how do you know when a door is still open and when it's clearly shut? Just when is God telling you to keep persevering and when to give up?

Perseverance Pays Off
One point is indisputable. Scripture abounds with examples

of those who found doors open at points when many would have concluded they were bolted shut. As we read through the Bible, we find numerous instances where individuals reached important horizons late in life, or after repeated tries, or in spite of extreme obstacles. Sarah conceives a child when both she and Abraham are elderly, and a number of years later Abraham remarries after Sarah dies. Isaac's servants dig a well successfully after two major thwarted attempts. Joseph realizes his dream of leadership after years of servitude and imprisonment. Moses becomes a champion of his people forty years after his first passionate attempt utterly fails. David becomes king of Israel in spite of severe ridicule from his brothers, apathy from his father and numerous battles with Saul's forces. Hannah gives birth to many children long after her husband has accepted her barrenness and encouraged her to do the same. Ruth finds joy in a new marriage after her first husband dies; and Naomi, bereft of her husband and both sons, finds unexpected solace in a grandchild born to Ruth. Zechariah and Elizabeth are blessed with a child in their old age, and the angel declares that this gift is in response to their longstanding prayers.

It's examples like these, I suspect, that lead author Garry Friesen to claim that the Bible doesn't recognize the concept of closed doors. I came across this point when reading his *Decision Making and the Will of God* and was intrigued by it. Friesen notes:

> Interestingly, though Christians today speak of doors that are "closed," Scripture does not. The need for open doors certainly implies the existence of some that are closed. But that doesn't seem to be the mentality of Paul. If he were sovereignly prevented from pursuing

a plan, and yet the plan itself was sound, he simply waited and tried again later. He did not view a blocked endeavor as a "closed door" sign from God that his plan was faulty.[1]

Friesen's claim is provocative, for on one level Scripture does speak of closed doors, though it does not use the term per se. Consider Paul's odyssey in Asia and Bithynia, for instance: "Paul and his companions traveled throughout the region of Phrygia and Galatia, having been kept by the Holy Spirit from preaching the word in the province of Asia. When they came to the border of Mysia, they tried to enter Bithynia, but the Spirit of Jesus would not allow them to" (Acts 16: 6-7). It's hard to read this passage and not conclude that some doors were firmly shut against Paul and his party, regardless of the language used. They made two valiant attempts to enter regions for ministry that didn't open to them. And they accepted without question that these doors were closed. "So they passed by Mysia and went down to Troas" (Acts 16:8).

Yet on a broader level the passage validates the very point Friesen is making, for Paul and his friends never let go of their overriding determination to evangelize fresh territory and to look for the best opportunities available for doing so. Soon Paul received a vision at night through which he and his team were led into a fruitful period of ministry in Macedonia (Acts 16:9-40).

Drawing on Paul's experience in Acts 16 and similar experiences of people of faith throughout Scripture, we can suggest a resolution to the question of when a door is truly closed. *Specific individual opportunities may close to us, and the time may come when we must accept that such doors are truly shut. But we should be very slow ever to conclude that the door is permanently closed against our broader, long-term aspirations that are based on a sound understanding of our God-given gifts and areas of interest.*

To cite the marriage decision as an example: I may desire to marry a certain person, and make a reasonable effort to win her affection, yet she says no and insists it's firm. I will need to accept this no as unequivocal and stop pounding on that door. God may say no to twenty such possibilities through this process! This doesn't mean that my basic, underlying desire to be married is inappropriate or that God is forever closing the door against marriage. Indeed, it may be that my twenty-first endeavor succeeds. To be sure, if there are clear lessons to be gleaned from past disappointments, I should learn them. Yet if I earnestly desire to be married, I still have a sound basis for staying hopeful and active in moving toward my dream.

The same point applies to pursuing career opportunities. Certain job positions may not open to me. Certain geographical regions may be closed. This doesn't imply that my overriding vocational aspirations are out of line. If they are based on a clear understanding of how God has gifted and motivated me, then I have good reason to hold on to them and to continue to look for situations in which they can be fulfilled.

Hope vs. Fixation

This isn't to underestimate the challenge involved in accepting that a specific door is closed. Indeed, we can become fixated on a particular option's working out to the point of our own downfall. One of the earliest stories of Scripture underscores this point. Adam and Eve became obsessed with eating fruit from the one tree God said they must not touch.

The fact that this tree was off limits didn't mean that God forbade them to enjoy apples or other delicacies of nature. It was merely that this *specific* tree was out of bounds for them.

In the same way we may become fixated on a particular relationship. We may continue to hang on to the hope of its working out long after we have clear evidence that this person is unavailable or unsuitable for us. In this case our need is to accept God's no and move on.

We can become fixated on other unrealistic dreams as well. I'll never forget a young man I met, Clarence—a singer-guitarist who led singing in his church. He was convinced God had told him he was going to receive a recording contract from a certain Christian record company, one of the largest and best-known firms. Even after the company rejected Clarence's audition tape, he continued to believe that he knew God's mind on the matter better than they did. He was sure they would one day change their mind and decide to record him. It did not seem to me, however, that Clarence had the distinctive sort of talent needed to interest a major record company. The tragedy about his obsession with the recording contract was that it misdirected his energy. He wasn't focusing on steps he realistically *could* take to develop and employ his gifts.

These cautions aside, the point remains that we have a strong basis for faith and hope when it comes to our long-term dreams and aspirations. When these are based on a good self-understanding and are general enough to allow for flexibility as they are fleshed out, we can feel great freedom to pursue them earnestly until a door finally opens. And we're not obliged to think that individual setbacks mean that God has forever shut the door on a dream itself.

Conclusion

In short, it makes enormous sense for us to set ambitious goals based on a good understanding of how God has gifted and energized us. Dreams that seem grandiose at arm's length so often can be accomplished when broken down into one or more carefully conceived goals. We may hesitate to take on such aspiring goals, fearing we're not competent enough to carry them out, or that we'll face obstacles too great to conquer. Yet appreciating the concept of horizontal time, as God's unspeakable gift for realizing our potential, helps us see that with patient persistence these goals can be achieved—and at a pace that's natural for us.

And, as we've stressed, we're not obligated to conclude that failures or setbacks signal that God is nixing our important goals or dreams. Individual options may close to us. Yet apart from a compelling reason to change course, we're free to continue wholeheartedly pursuing our broader aspirations. And we best honor God through this persistence.

To this end, I strongly hope our discussion in this short book has inspired you to take your personal dreams more seriously. I genuinely believe that if you start putting goals into motion following the strategy I outlined in chapter one, that you'll find yourself capable of achievements vastly exceeding what you've ever imagined. And you'll accomplish them at a pace that is relaxed and natural for you. Once you do set a goal correctly, the key to achieving it lies in staying with it long enough to reach it. I hope the last two chapters have inspired the "stick-to-itiveness" so needed to follow a goal through to the finish.

If you would like further direction and encouragement toward realizing your dreams, I've recently published a full book on this subject: *Reach Beyond Your Grasp: Embracing Dreams That Reflect God's Best for You—And Achieving Them.* If your dream is to find someone to marry, I've published a book on that recently as well: *Marry a Friend: Finding Someone to Marry Who Is Truly Right for You.*

In concluding, I urge you not to play it safe with your life, but to be willing to take reasonable risks. Remember that walking in faith means moving ahead in the face of some doubts and fears. If you wait until you feel perfectly comfortable about taking an important step, you'll wait forever, and your dream will never materialize. Go ahead and put that dream on the front burner. Pray earnestly for Christ's direction. Then map out your strategy in some carefully planned goals, and move ahead. Then stay with that dream until you reach it. I wish you God's very greatest blessings as you consider which new adventure to pursue and then go for it. And may he grant you the grace to realize your highest potential for Christ!!!

Appendix

Overcoming Your Fears of Change

If you have an important goal or dream you dearly want to pursue, but are having trouble getting started, fears of change may be holding back. This chapter from my Faith and Optimism *addresses the problem. I hope these thoughts will give you the heart to put that dream or goal on the front burner!*

IN THE DAYS LEADING UP to my ordination service, I was surprised to find that I dreaded the occasion as much as I looked forward to it. While I knew that important benefits would come from being ordained, the thought of taking the step frightened me. I feared that I didn't deserve the honor and wouldn't be able to handle the increased sense of significance it would bring.

Yet once the service was over and the formalities past—once there was no easy turning back—I suddenly felt at home with my new status. Never, in fact, during the forty years since have I wavered in feeling comfortable with the distinction of being ordained, which in its own way has served to open many doors.

We may experience a multitude of fears when making a major personal change. We can fear success as much as failure, and—in relationships—commitment as much as rejection. So often, though, the heart of the problem is simply that *we don't like change.* When we look carefully at what frightens us, we find it is the fear of change that is holding us back.

This was clearly the case as I approached my ordination ceremony. Becoming ordained meant letting go of a comfortable old identity for an uncertain new one. And it meant growing up a bit, opening myself to new responsibilities. And that was scary.

Let's face it. Change of any sort—whether modest or major—can be unnerving to us. As journalist Ellen Goodman notes,

> We cling to even the minor routines with an odd tenacity. We're upset when the waitress who usually brings us coffee in the breakfast shop near the office suddenly quits, and are disoriented if the drugstore or the cleaner's in the neighborhood closes. . . . We each have a litany of holiday rituals and everyday habits that we hold on to, and we often greet radical innovation with the enthusiasm of a baby meeting a new sitter.[1]

Of course we find unwelcome change unsettling. But this can be just as true when the change is one we strongly desire to make. That is to say, we can long for the change on one level yet fear it on another. Such ambivalence when making a major change is extremely common, although most people are surprised when they experience it. This vexing mixture of emotions is reflected by a comment in a recent news article on the trauma of changing your lifestyle: "Here

I am, moving into a permanent relationship and we've just bought a wonderful new house. So why do I find selling my smaller condo so wrenching?"[2]

Not a few Christians are startled to experience such divided feelings after making a decision to marry. On at least eight occasions in the last year alone, Christians have sought my counsel due to cold feet after becoming engaged. One brilliant, mature Christian man went through three major episodes of doubt during the two months before his wedding, even though he had made the commitment to marry with great conviction of heart. In another case, a woman was ready to cancel her wedding on only ten days' notice. She had earnestly desired to marry this man and at the time of her engagement was certain that God was leading her to do so. Yet as their wedding day approached, her apprehensions grew to the point of practically overriding her better judgment.

As my ordination experience demonstrates, though, the fears we experience in the face of a major change are often deceptive. They are aggravated by our knowing that we still have the freedom to change our mind. Once we take the step and are no longer free to renege, they usually vanish. In the case of marriage, it typically happens that after the vows are taken and the festivities are over, the fears that were so disabling are forgotten.

We go through this identical process in other changes as well. Taking a decisive step is usually necessary to put our fears to rest.

Perfect Peace?
Complicating the matter for many Christians, though, is an

unfortunate notion about Christ's peace. Many assume that if God is leading you to do something, you'll experience perfect peace. This is usually thought to mean that no fears or doubts will intrude: If you have any misgivings at all about taking the step, then God is warning you not to go ahead.

While Scripture teaches that Christ gives peace to those who follow him, it never guarantees that we will *feel* peaceful as we begin to take a step forward. God doesn't overrule our psyche. The peace that he gives, rather, enables us to *transcend* our fears—to move ahead in spite of many hesitations. We may feel a mixture of peace and fear at the same time, especially in the early stages of making a major change. Many of us are so constituted psychologically that we simply cannot feel peaceful *in advance* of a major step but only afterward. Taking the step is vital to experiencing Christ's peace and opening ourselves to the full blessings of God.

Indeed, faith often involves the resolve to move ahead in spite of fear.

The Lure of the Comfort Zone

The call of Moses provides a helpful example of these principles. When God confronted Moses through the burning bush, he offered him an exceptional opportunity to do something meaningful with his life. Yet Moses responded with extreme fear and reluctance: "Who am I, that I should go to Pharaoh and bring the Israelites out of Egypt? . . . 0 Lord, please send someone else to do it" (Ex 3:11; 4:13).

We could easily conclude that Moses didn't really want the position that God was offering him. As a young man, though, he had displayed exactly the aspirations which this position would now fulfill. His passion to free his fellow

Jews from oppression was so great that it spurred him to murder an Egyptian whom he caught abusing an Israelite (Ex 2:11-12). In all likelihood this zeal was still inside of him, though it had been repressed for decades.

Fear of repercussions after he killed the Egyptian led Moses to seek refuge in the desert. For forty years he worked as a shepherd and lived in the home of a respected priest. We may guess that while life was not bristling with adventure for Moses during this time, it was not terribly stressful either. When God finally asked Moses to deliver Israel, Moses expressed intense fears of failure. Yet undoubtedly he feared change as well, for accepting the call would mean leaving a number of familiar comforts.

Interestingly, as Moses responded to God's call, he not only realized dramatic success but experienced remarkable fulfillment too. Not that it was easy. He was stretched and challenged enormously. Yet through the whole process came times of unparalleled intimacy with God, substantial growth in his leadership skills, and the radical joy of knowing that his life was accomplishing something noteworthy. We might add that his long-term physical vitality probably benefited as well, for at the time of his death at the age of one hundred twenty, "his eyes were not weak nor his strength gone" (Deut 34:7).

Taking Control

Perhaps you are considering a major change. It may be a career move or a new educational pursuit. Or a change in your living situation. Or a step forward in a relationship—or the breaking off of one. Or a change in your church affiliation, or a new venture in using your gifts within your church.

You may have approached this decision carefully and prayerfully and have good reason to believe that God is prompting you to go ahead. At the same time you're dogged with doubts and fears and a general uneasiness about making any change at all. If so, let me suggest five points of perspective to keep in mind:

1. Second thoughts are normal. No matter how mature you are spiritually and how diligently you have sought God's will, it is still common to have second thoughts about your decision. Yes, you may look with envy on friends who leap into marriage with perfect confidence that they have found God's choice, or on those who make career changes with surreal assurance that they're following God's will. Remember, though, that you are constructed differently psychologically than they are. You may even be a deeper thinker. And they may be ignoring misgivings which will come out later in more damaging ways. Be thankful that you recognize your feelings and don't repress them.

Remember, too, that Scripture is full of people, like Moses, who took major steps in the face of considerable ambivalence yet were clearly following God's will. Accept your psychological makeup for what it is.

2. Take time to mourn what you are leaving behind. No matter how greatly you desire to make this change, you're still letting go of certain cherished benefits in order to do it. The person eager for marriage, for instance, is relinquishing the treasured freedom of single life and forsaking forever the possibility of considering another option for an intimate relationship. Even when the change brings unquestioned improvements to your life, it's still normal to feel grief over what you're leaving behind. Don't be ashamed to face up to this. Take time to feel your grief and work through it. But don't let it hold you back from moving on to God's best.

3. Pray for strength and eagerness. While prayer has many purposes in Scripture, one of the most essential is to gain courage when taking a major step of faith. Jesus gave us a vivid demonstration of this in Gethsemane. Through an hour or so of earnest prayer his outlook was transformed, and he gained the determination and confidence he needed to proceed with his mission. Give some dedicated time to praying about your decision. But don't merely ask for guidance—ask for strength and eagerness to take the course that is best for you. Praying in this fashion can make a significant difference.

4. Take control of your psyche. You have considerably more control than you probably realize over the mood swings which accompany a major personal change. The people with whom you associate, for instance, affect your outlook dramatically. There may be those who, regardless of their intentions, find it difficult to feel positive about the change you want to make. Their own identity is tied to how you are now. For you to change means adjustments for them too—in their routine, in their pattern of relating to you, in how they see themselves. They may not do anything overtly to discourage you from moving ahead. Still, it is difficult to be around them and not feel guilty for upsetting the equilibrium in their lives. You wonder if you should be making any change at all.

Others will be much more forward-looking in the way they see you. They are able to think beyond their own narrow concerns and appreciate what God is doing in your life. They trust your judgment and share your excitement for taking on new adventures and risks. And they genuinely want to see you succeed. They reflect the supremely supportive spirit which David displays in Psalm 20: "May [God] give you the desire of your heart and make all your plans succeed. We will shout for joy when you are victorious and will lift up our banners in the name of our God. May the LORD grant all your requests" (vv 4-5).

Don't forsake those who find it hard to agree with you. But give priority to spending time with those who are able to think creatively about your life. Their perspective will be contagious. Remember that Jesus himself chose to move away from Nazareth into settings where people's expectations of him were higher. This suggests that we should consider it a point of stewardship to avoid too much contact with negative people. We benefit most by being with those who see us dynamically.

5. *Accept the principle of tradeoffs.* The modern belief that we can "have it all" subtly affects our outlook as Christians. While Scripture promises that Christ's blessings during this life are immense, though, it teaches that there are always tradeoffs involved in embracing them. Challenging choices must be made to let go of one benefit in order to enjoy another. Once we accept this—and that perfection is never possible in our choices—it becomes easier to take steps forward. Change itself becomes less threatening.

We may not be able to overcome our fundamental uneasiness with change. Still, we don't have to let our fears of change be the controlling factor in the decisions we make, or the final word in our life. There is much we can do to break the grip of these fears, and these outlooks I've suggested can help greatly.

The best news is that God is on your side as you make the effort to confront your fears of change and embrace his best for you. Be *determined* in this effort, trusting that he will give you all the grace you need as you step forward. May God grant you the wisdom to see his best at every point in your life, and the courage to move beyond any fears that stand in the way!

Notes

Chapter 2: The Triumph of Simple Persistence

[1]Napoleon Hill shares this story in *Think and Grow Rich* (Hollywood: Melvin Powers Wilshire Book Co., 1966), pp. 20-21. While I don't embrace Hill's philosophy at every point, his book contains many compelling examples, like this one, of individuals who overcame serious obstacles (real or perceived) in accomplishing personal goals, as well as good practical advice about goal setting.

[2]Gene N. Landrum, Ph.D., *Eight Keys to Greatness: How to Unlock Your Hidden Potential* (Amherst, NY: Prometheus Books, 1999), p. 191.

[3]Ibid., p. 200.

[4]Keith Ellis, *The Magic Lamp: Goal Setting for People Who Hate Setting Goals* (NY: Three Rivers Press, 1998), pp. 69ff. Ellis's book is the best I have seen on setting and achieving personal goals.

[5]Ibid., p. 71.

Chapter 3: When Is a Door Truly Closed?
[1]Garry Friesen with J. Robin Maxson, *Decision Making and the Will of God: A Biblical Alternative to the Traditional View* (Portland, Ore.: Multnomah, 1980), p. 221.

Addendum: Confronting the Fear of Change
[1]Ellen Goodman, *Turning Points: How People Change Through Crisis and Commitment* (New York: Fawcett Crest, 1979), p. 15.
[2]Susan Porter Robinson, "In a Period of Transition," *The Washington Post,* March 22, 1990, Style section.

About the Author

Blaine Smith, a Presbyterian pastor, spent thirty years as director of Nehemiah Ministries, Inc., a resource ministry based in the Washington, D.C. area. He retired the organization in 2009, but continues to use the name Nehemiah Ministries for free-lance work.

His career has included giving seminars and lectures, speaking at conferences, counseling, and writing. He is author of ten books, including *Marry a Friend, Knowing God's Will* (original and revised editions), *Should I Get Married?* (original and revised editions), *The Yes Anxiety, Overcoming Shyness, Faith and Optimism* (originally *The Optimism Factor), One of a Kind, Reach Beyond Your Grasp,* and *Emotional Intelligence for Christians,* as well as numerous articles. These books have been published in more than thirty English language and international editions. He is also lecturer for *Guidance By The Book,* a home study course with audio cassettes produced by the Christian Broadcasting Network as part of their *Living By The Book* series.

Blaine served previously as founder/director of the Sons of Thunder, believed by many to be America's first active Christian rock band, and as assistant pastor of Memorial Presbyterian Church in St. Louis. He is an avid guitarist, and currently performs with the Newports, an oldies band.

Blaine is a graduate of Georgetown University, and also holds a Master of Divinity from Wesley Theological Seminary and a Doctor of Ministry from Fuller Theological Seminary. He and Evie live in Gaithersburg, Maryland. They've been married since 1973, and have two grown sons, Benjamin and Nathan. Ben and his wife Lorinda have two children, Jackson Olen (2009) and Marlena Mae (2012).

Blaine also authors a twice-monthly online newsletter, *Nehemiah Notes*, featuring a practical article on the Christian faith, posted on his ministry website and available by e-mail for free.

You may e-mail Blaine at mbs@nehemiahministries.com.

Made in the USA
Lexington, KY
14 November 2012